The Water of Life

Bringing Healing to People and Spirits with Heavenly Forces

Ars Aurora

Copyright © 2021 Ars Aurora

No part of this book may be reproduced, stored, or posted in any form or by any means, without the express permission of the author.

The information in this book is for educational purposes only and is not intended for treatment, diagnosis, or prescription of any diseases. This book is not intended to provide financial or health advice of any kind. The author is in no way responsible for any improper use of the material in this book. No guarantee of results is being made in this book.

Any act that may inflict copyright, is subject to legal action.

If you got into this book by buying an official copy, or offered at official and regulated distributors, I bless you by all the heavenly forces in this universe, and may you have always, everything you want, by the divine mercy of Archangel Tzadkiel, forever and ever, amen.

I dedicate this book to all the luminous spirits who aim to ascend the Earth in their love and mercy.

Thank you, beloved Archangel Michael, for all the love received.

- Introduction 8
- The water of life 9
- Divine properties 10
- Manifesting Healing by Angels 13
- The four pillars 14
- The angelic forces 17
- Honorable mentions 20
- Two methods of Blessing 21
- The Blessing of the water of life 22
- Angelic Seal of Healing 24
- Celestial Oil 25
- Celestial Candle 28
- Celestial incense 29
- The Fountain of Life 30
- Final notes 34

Introduction

In this book, I will teach you a simple technique that can revolutionize your contacts with any desired entity, that is a process of healing, of love, of gratitude, and of respect for all the entities that help us in our earthly journey.

The water of life, as it was called by Daimon Orobas in my contacts with him, was the fruit of my approach with all the spirits I have contact with. Always aiming at love, healing, ascension, illumination, and liberation from the pains that each one may suffer.

During a walk of spiritual healing, something welled up inside my spirit, endless questions and questions about the experience and pain that each spirit feels, and how I could help each one to have more peace in their existence, and it was from these questions that I developed this simple technique, the water of life, which moves cosmic forces in benefit of those who drink it, and being a process of healing and intention, it helps each one of those who receive it, in their physical and spiritual journeys.

The water of life

Water, in our history and through various religions and cultures throughout this world, is the primordial symbol of life, healing, and purification, and as an element that instantly absorbs the vibrations and forces around it, it is a perfect element for driving a practitioner's spiritual intention and will.

Holistic therapists, and people who have the knowledge of the vibrations and forces around us, are used to the simple technique of energizing a glass with water to heal physical and spiritual ailments.

To a thirsty spirit, would you give a cup of alcoholic drink or a cup of water?

For someone, who has wandered for several days in a burning desert, all that person wants is an oasis, with a fountain of fresh water to quench his thirst.

We can see the importance of this element on our earth; there is no nature without water, no crops, no animals, no food, and much less, life.

Divine properties

The water of life manifests healing forces and illumination to all who drink from it, in a gradual process of healing for all physical and spiritual pains and torments:

1° Healing of physical and spiritual pains.

On the physical plane, it can be used to help in the treatment of physical diseases, to bring relief to body pains, and to help in the recovery process from illnesses.

On the spiritual plane, water can stop body pains and wounds, heal wounds, and bring the regeneration of the spirit to the one who drinks it.

2° Spiritual enlightenment.

On the physical and spiritual planes, it can increase the vibration level of the person, because the same person will be ingesting in his/her physical body a celestial blessing and force, which will consequently increase the vibratory and energetic pattern of the person.

On the spiritual plane in particular, the water brings along with it the divine blessings of the angels to which it was consecrated. The spirit that ingests this force receives light, and this light illuminates its life and existence, setting in motion a constant process of healing and evolution, if it constantly or periodically drinks from this ambrosia.

3° Vivification of the spirit.

On both the physical and spiritual planes, this water can bring the life force, the life that pulsates over all of us, the life that makes the divine virtues manifest, truly being a light that brings celestial vibrations and energies.

Spirits that do not have in their spiritual bodies the chakras completely formed, or those such as elementals, enchanted spirits (who have not gone through an incarnational experience), or those who need a source of energy to survive, as for example spiritual servants, this water has the power to energize, give strength, power, life, and resistance to these spirits, especially in elementals and unborn beings that are not energetically connected to any human being, which is the case of artificial servants. In the case of elementals and unborn beings, water acts to increase and intensify the evolutionary process, giving sacred properties and divine blessings to those who drink it.

4° Release of pains and negative ties.

On the physical plane, it has the same effect and action in the treatment and recovery from pain and illness.

On the spiritual plane, where its action is more intensified and illuminated, it can free the spirit from negative realities and forces that bring pain and suffering to it. Imagine you are offering water, whose power is blessed by the divine forces of healing and illumination to every creature, and a spirit whose existence and a spirit whose existence is surrounded by pain, suffering, storms, and negative ties, you are giving him liberation, the water will go through the spirit of the one who took it, transmuting, liberating, and vivifying the one who takes it, thus, breaking the infinite cycles of pain that he may have in his spiritual journey.

I believe that with this information, you can realize that the technique and blessing of the water of life is the greatest and best gift that can be offered to those who need its properties, regardless of who they are, and that it is a vehicle of healing and spiritual ascension for everyone who drinks it.

Although it is relatively simple to do, everything is symbolic, for a small gesture of love can become a great spiritual change.

Manifesting Healing by Angels

Angels are forces that can act on behalf of all spirits on this earth, of all pantheons, cultures, religions, and forces that manifest, for example ancestral spirits, family members, gods and goddesses, daimons, demons, elementals, and unborn forces are great examples of the scope of this technique. These denominations of "angel, god, daemon, demon, unborn beings, elementals" are just ways of categorizing and even mystifying what in essence is a spirit, like any other, in different evolutionary and vibratory stages. Just like you and me.

The forces of healing, love, mercy, and enlightenment are universal, and do not belong to any specific human being or entity. There is no single and exclusive holder of these energies on our earth, or in our constellation, the angels are a way to conduct and manifest these cosmic forces in favor of whomever we wish.

In ancient times, before any book of magic was released or written, before any dogma or norm was created to control angelic contact, humanity was much more connected to spirituality, there was not this illusory separation that we have today, spiritual contact was easily accessible and constant, just reflect on the ancient stories, With time, mankind lost the ability to interact with the spiritual world, and with this loss, the human being had to reinvent himself to once again be able to access the subtle planes of spirituality.

The four pillars

The four pillars are points that I practice and base myself, I faithfully believe, and my positive results only reinforce my theory, that the best way to work with any entity is based on four points or four pillars that I will exemplify below, and having a fifth pillar or hidden point, which is extremely crucial for things not to get out of control.

Love

Love is a very wide energy, and can hardly be written in small words, love is not loving someone for what he or she does for you, this is love attached to the ego, the purest love, it is unconditional love, which loves regardless of the situations.

Respect

Respect is the basis of any physical and spiritual relationship, no one likes to be around or live with people who are rude, discriminating, racist, and much less to be around those who think they are bigger and better than others. In contact with any entity, if you maintain a line of respect, being educated, cordial, and kind to every creature, every entity will be much more likely to help you, use empathy and put yourself in the other's place.

Gratitude

To be grateful for the conversation you had with the spirit, to be grateful for the help received, to be grateful for every feeling of comfort and peace received during the ritual, being grateful for the one who free you from physical and spiritual evil, free you from pain and suffering, and rise up again through the necessary painful lessons of life.

Humbleness

Humility is based entirely on not thinking you own the reason, the power, and the sovereignty against anyone, being humble and respecting the force that you called on to help you is one of the most beautiful ways to enrich the contact with any desired spirit. Being humble is not submission, it is not being a slave, it is not blind worship, and much less letting your life be controlled by the wishes of others, you are not lowering your head or submitting to anyone.

And finally, one last secret point and the most crucial of all:

Maintain control in every situation.

There are spirits of various polarities, vibrations and energies in this world, you must never allow any of them to disrespect you, it is not because you are being humble and respectful with them that they will have the facility to do whatever they wish with your life. Always impose limits, barriers and forces for your own wellbeing.

The lack of imposed limits is always the biggest mistake in social relationships, from small hidden acts that aim to diminish life or a person "innocently", to big actions that are clearly toxic and wrong, this applies in all possible relationships, and should be applied in your relationships with spiritual entities and with all the people around you, in your cycle of friendship and family.

The secret is to have the balance, in respecting the entity, but at the same time, being able to have control in case things can go wrong, there are several spiritual forms that can help you in this matter, spirits linked to order, protection and justice are wonderful. For me, Archangel Michael is the best.

The angelic forces

The blessings attributed to the water of life are based on certain and very specific angelic forces, each angel has its own action to bring enlightenment and the ceasing of pains and torments, and that is why this simple offering is so appreciated by the spirits that receive it, these angels are:

Metatron: In my fifteen years of study and practice with angel magic, I have never met or known an Archangel like Metatron, it is amazing his manifestations and forces universe, this archangel is gigantic in his form, strength and energy, for the same is the living symbol of the "Cube of Metatron", he also has his over existence the symbol "Merkabah", both are sacred symbols pulsating in life, and are universal, they manifest in all cosmos, not only in this solar system.

Metatron has under his regency the ascension and spiritual illumination to every creature, freeing and healing existences from all pains, sufferings and torments, besides irradiating infinitely the celestial and divine blessings, that is why his honor is so great and his action is so beneficial to all those who receive it, he is always the Archangel that I conjure to bless the water of life, the primordial life that illuminates every creature, it is an applied symbology, you are giving something that will vivify and bless the one who takes it.

Mahashel: Mahashel is one of the 72 kabbalistic angels, also known as the angel of the Shem HaMephorash, this angel has over his performance, the healing in its total scope, however, he holds a very specific type of performance that I consider crucial, which is the healing of the soul and emotional pain, when conjuring this force, you will be energizing the water with a quality of internal healing on all who take it.

Rehoel: Rehoel is one of the 72 kabbalistic angels, also known as the angel of the Shem HaMephorash, he has under his regency the transmutation of all things, just like Metatron, Rehoel can transmute situations, pains, torments, negative aspects, energies, forces and physical/spiritual/dimensional realities, he holds this particular aspect that can go through past lives, and act on all levels and spiritual dimensions in favor of those who call for it, by calling this force to bless the water of life, you will be starting a process of timeless healing and transmutation of old, present and future pains.

Rafael: Raphael is the regent archangel of the sun, she brings the solar illumination and its beneficial qualities over all this earth, in her many descriptions and reports, she acts on the healing of all disease of this earth, besides possessing many beneficial qualities for all those who work with her, for being the most known archangel to heal pains, Raphael is perfect to bring and manifest the creative and universal energies of healing over all situation, she is also very much recognized on other planets, planes, constellations and spiritual dimensions, for she was the only one who could uncover and create life in the same way the primordial source/creator did at the beginning of time, information that I believe no one knows until now, for this great achievement, she is honored and exalted in her knowledge, studies and wisdom.

Orfaniel: Orfaniel is a great angel for healing and spiritual cleansing. He works very well to remove the forces that cause sickness and disease in a person. His name "Orf" is derived from the Hebrew word for "light". He is described in works as an angel capable of bringing illumination and healing feelings.

These are the main forces of this healing work, and a simple conjuration of all of them already has the desired effect on the water. It is all a matter of adding energy to what you are going to bless and consecrate, this is an act of respect, love, and consideration with the one you are going to call, or even with your family, relatives, friends, or anyone you are going to give this water to drink.

Do not be attached to the idea of offering this water only to spirits, it can and should be used in your daily life, to help in the treatment of pains, diseases, regeneration of the spiritual bodies, as well as to confer celestial blessings.

Honorable mentions

The water of life, is just a simple and great example, that a symbolic act imbued with faith, love, respect, empathy and mercy, can completely change the way you relate to any person or desired entity, a glass of consecrated water, is just one example of Blessing, you can use this same example to consecrate objects, food, candles, incense, the possibilities are endless.

If you are a student of magic with angels, or have a reliable source of angelic performances, you can adapt the conjurations and forces called for so that they have the desired properties in your Blessing, for example:

Menakel: To manifest forgiveness.

Yeretel: To break ties, cords, ropes, pacts, vows, and physical and spiritual bonds.

Mihel: To manifest divine mercy, love and light.

Tzadkiel: To manifest kindness and mercy.

Vehuael: To cleanse the heart of sorrows and darkness.

These are just small examples, the Blessing process is always the same, asking the angel or force in question, to attribute and bless the water/food/candle/object/incense and whatever you desire.

Two methods of Blessing

There are two ways to consecrate water, the first way, which is the simplest and which I have used as an offering for all entities, the second method, is used with an angelic seal to energize and potentiate the water and the Blessing.

The angelic seal of the second method, is basically and completely focused only on the angelic forces, the divine names of Christ is used to radiate the beneficial forces, but who does the blessing and the Blessing is the angels and mainly you.

I particularly only use the angelic seal to energize and bless water for individuals to drink, such as leaving the angelic seal under the water filter, or under a glass of water to be drunk later.

It is important to emphasize that in this simple but great act, we must use universal forces, and not earthly ones, and definitely not use entities or deities that have had in their history, war processes, destruction of other faiths and cultures. The divine, Christic and sacred forces are always the most recommended to manifest healing through this act of kindness.

The Blessing of the water of life

Take a clean glass/cup/bowl and fill it up to the top with filtered water, it can't be tap water, the water needs to be clean from impurities in the plumbing, place your two clean hands holding the glass/cup/bowl, preferably holding at chest height, and say the following Blessing:

"In the name of the Christ, by the power of the Christ, by the glory and splendor of the Christ. I bless, consecrate, and give you life, creature of water, by the same life that flows in the celestial rivers, by the name and power of Metatron, may everyone who drinks from you, have his thirst quenched, and have his body, spirit, life, and entire existence, in all levels, dimensions and interdimensional realities, healed, from all pains, all wounds, all sores, by the force and cosmic manifestation of healing, kindness, love, and mercy, and by the forces and actions of the healing angels, Mahashel who heals every soul, Rehoel who transmutes every pain, Raphael who heals and illuminates every life, and Orfaniel who battles against every suffering, and by the divine blessings of the Archangel Metatron, from eternity to eternity, forever and ever, amen."

Now just offer the water to the desired entity.

The water doesn't necessarily need to be in a cup or with a bowl, it can be an ordinary cup, preferably made of glass, because plastic doesn't conduct energy, the cup/glass/bowl can be used normally if you can't afford a specific, for the entity or your magical works.

To use the Blessing with the angelic seal, the process is the same, just print or draw the angelic seal of healing, place the bowl/cup of water on top of the seal, and say the Blessing that was taught on the previous page, and after that, offer the water to the desired entity, removing the seal of healing from the ritual.

The angelic seal can also be placed under the water filter, under your bed, pillow, on your door, or in any desired place (except in bathrooms or dirty environments), so that it irradiates healing and beneficial energies to the people who live there.

Angelic Seal of Healing

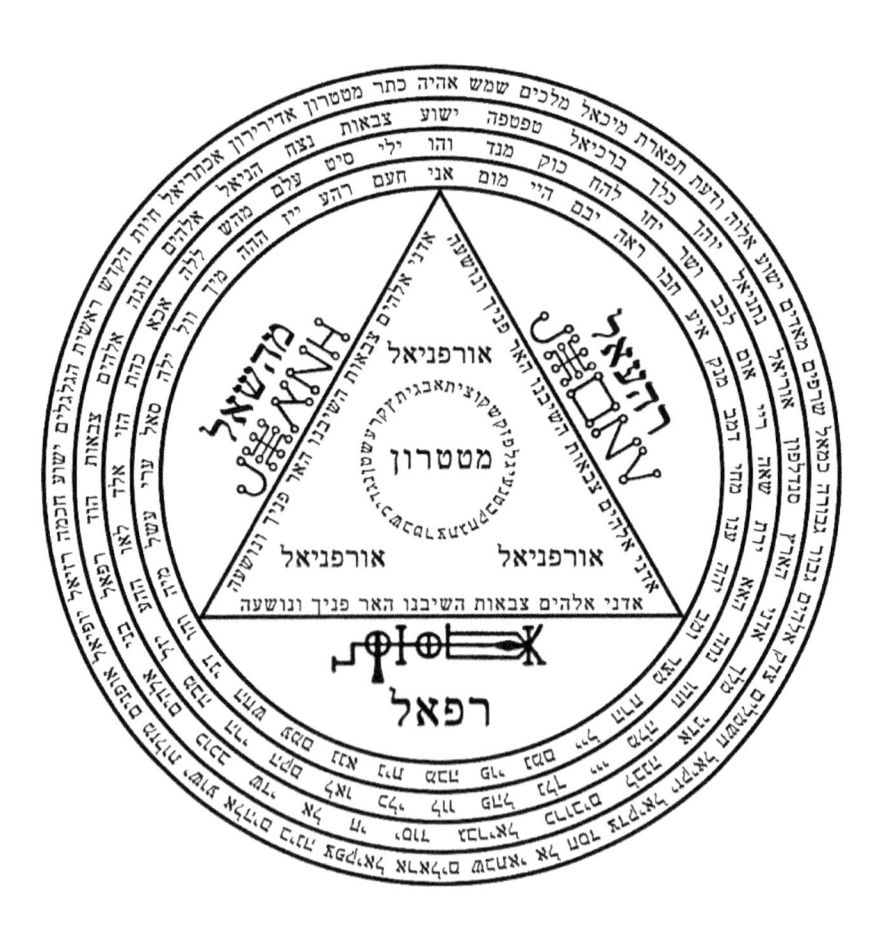

Celestial Oil

Celestial oil, is a mixture of three elements well known in the world of magic, often used in incenses and smokers, Myrrh, Frankincense and Balsam.

These aromatic elements have sacred and symbolic properties, Myrrh and Frankincense were used as offerings when Jesus Christ came to life, and the Three Kings already knew of the divine properties of these elements, their use brings the forces of healing, calm, peace, meditation, and balance.

Balsam is often cited in Biblical manuscripts as that which purifies and heals, drives away sorrows and bad vibrations.

The combination of these three elements forms a powerful oil that can be used to anoint and consecrate the candles, the way I will teach you, is focused on blessing and illumination, just like the water of life, this oil will also have divine blessing and healing properties.

On the next page, I will leave the instructions that were also passed on in my book "Angelic Magick, rituals and conjurations with the celestial angels".

The recipe for heavenly oil that can be used for all rituals of magick with angels, and with daimons is:

- Extra virgin olive oil or sunflower oil.

(Only if you use the dried herbs/plants).

- Myrrh.

- Frankincense.

- Balsam.

Myrrh, Frankincense and Balsam, you can use either the dried herbs/ plants or the natural oils and mix them, the portion is the same for all ingredients, just mix them and keep them in a recipient.

If you use dried herbs, you must filter the mixture in 7 days, leaving only the oil, but this is relative from tradition to tradition, as always, follow your intuition.

When the oil is ready, say this following prayer over it, to consecrate it to magical practices.

"I bless, consecrate, and give you life, creature of the oil, by its sacred and divine properties attributed to you, by the strength and name of Metatron, prince of the divine presence, by the strength and power of the stars and of this universe, by the strength and power of mercy, love, peace and redemption and enlightenment of every creature, may everyone who is touched by you, be blessed and enlightened, and have his existence enlightened and all torment ceased, from eternity to eternity, forever and ever, so be it".

Just make this simple and powerful prayer, and light a purple, yellow, or white candle in front of the oil, which moves unimaginable forces for those who receive it, and, the oil will be ready for use, bathe the candles with the oil in all your magical operations, it can be used both for angels, daimons, spirits, gods, and goddesses, for any desire, intent, and operation that you will perform.

(This oil is not used to conjure up spiritual attacks against people and/or their enemies, because its action is to bless, and not to curse).

The way to bathe the candle is very simple:

- For requests and operations where you want to have something, achieve, manifest anything in your favor, bathe the candle from the wick of the candle, where the flame burns, to the base of the candle, where it stands upright, from top to bottom.

- For requests and operations where you want to get rid of something, destroy it, banish it, drive it away, you must bathe the candle from the base of the candle, where it stands, to the wick, where it lights, from the bottom to the top.

(In some traditions, the way of anointing the candle is the other way around, if you do it this way, follow your traditions).

Celestial Candle

The candle can also be a great bridge of strength and intention, depending on the way it is conjured and blessed, a correctly consecrated candle has unimaginable power, I will leave below a candle Blessing, so that it is offered to the spirits of your cult, in this Blessing, we always focus on manifesting peace and mercy to the one who will receive. You can use the same example below to consecrate your candles according to your needs, when, for example, you are going to do a ritual that will not offer anything to any entity, but rather use your own strength and power to manifest your will.

The conjuration and candle Blessing, I use in conjunction with the heavenly oil, you can adapt the conjuration if you cannot have or make the recipe of this oil, the blessing will always be strong, according to your faith, the conjuration is as follows:

"I bless, consecrate, and I give you life, creature of the candle and creature of the fire that will be formed, by this blessed and sacred oil, by the power and name of Metatron, may you go through all the firmaments of this earth and the heavens, go through all the stars, constellations and cosmos of this universe, in all levels, dimensions, planes and spiritual realities, and bring the liberation of all pain and suffering of the one who receives you, may your strength be irradiated, with your eternal flames, which are manifested over all things, may your light illuminate all darkness and suffering, may your flames warm all cold, and may your blessings be manifested eternally, in favor of all the one you are offered, forever and ever, from eternity to eternity, by the strength and name of Metatron, amen".

Celestial incense

Incense brings fragrance and sacred properties, which manifest themselves and drive away all bad odors. As there was no running water, baths were only taken at certain times of the year, and even then, hygiene was very precarious, incense was also used to disguise the bad smell of the places where the ancient magicians performed their rituals.

In addition to these curiosities, incense has the ability to alter the physical and spiritual space where it is accessed.

The best incense sticks without a doubt are the natural ones, but they are more expensive and not accessible to all people. I recommend you read the descriptions of the materials it is made of, and if you have essential oil from the plant/herb, you can use it freely, because it is very good and the spirits appreciate.

The incense conjuration is:

"I bless, consecrate, and give you life, creature of the air, by the power and name of Metatron, may you perfume all the path and existence of the spirit that receives you, may your perfume be eternal, and may your divine properties echo throughout the universe, from eternity to eternity, forever and ever, amen".

The Fountain of Life

The Fountain of Life is a technique that has the same divine and sacred properties as the water of life, and its action has proven to be so immeasurable and impactful in the lives of spirits, that I strongly encourage every reader to perform this operation with all the spirits that you have contact with.

This divine fountain is a constant flow of light and healing that is manifested in favor of everyone you wish. The technique is based on the creation and manifestation of a fountain that flows the water of life infinitely, in the resting places of these entities on the spiritual plane or in other places that you want, not limited to space/time or distance, and can be created on other planets and galactic systems as well, after all, the force of kindness, healing, and enlightenment access all the portals of this universe.

To create this water source for the spirits, the process is very simple:

1° Get in touch with the desired entity, the best way to do this is in meditation, close your eyes and start connecting with the desired force, visualize its shape, its seal/sign, feel its energy, let this moment flow.

2° When you feel that you have established a connection with the spirit in question, ask to be guided to the creation of the fountain of life, in the place desired by this entity, the spirit will take you mentally and spiritually to the place where the fountain will be created.

2.1° In this process, all you have to do is believe in whatever will be shown to your mind, be it images, sensations, sounds, intuitions, or even impressions of a place, you may have a quick sensation of seeing or feeling something, such as a field, a cave, a mountain, a tree, a lava field, being inside a star or on a planet unknown to you, the beauty of this technique is the ability to take you without limits or barriers to any place on the spiritual plane. You don't necessarily need to see clearly, or feel clearly, the only certainty is that you will know when you are in the appropriate and desired location of the entity.

2.2° I also leave a precatory note to all the people who are going to perform this technique, with the constant changes on this earth, many spirits are manifesting in this world in false garb. Passing themselves off as something they are not. Think well and analyze these situations so as not to open negative portals with these entities in your life, someone who manifests himself through illusions and lies, one must remain cautious.

3° After being in the place desired by the entity from which you want to open the fountain of life, just visualize a fountain of water being created from this place, you can imagine and visualize a white marble fountain being created and manifested in the indicated place or the water comes directly from the earth, from a mountain, from a tree, the possibilities are infinite, you will feel inside your heart which method will be the most appropriate in this case, if you have doubts, opt for the creation of a beautiful white marble fountain that flows abundantly and infinitely a crystalline and pure water, you must keep this visualization for some moments, preferably minutes, or when you feel that the fountain was manifested in the spiritual plane.

4° The final step, is to perform the blessing and Blessing of the water of life, the process is the same as taught in the chapter indicated, extend your hands towards this source, say the prayer, you will see that the source will flow water whose strength has healing and divine properties, many times, the water becomes so pure, that it shines in contrast with shades of gold and white.

And so ends the process of the fountain of life, now the desired entity will infinitely have a fountain of healing water at its disposal, the fountain of life and the water of life do not replace each other, keep doing the same process with the water of life in all your contacts with the desired entities.

The process to create this fountain in specific places in the spiritual planes is the same, just visualize and mentalize the desired place, and do the same process, I strongly recommend you be guided by some reliable force in this case, so that you can open this fountain in crucial points, your faith will manifest planetary and cosmic miracles, don't forget that, opening this fountain in strategic points in planets, can change the course of evolution and healing of an entire planetary system.

The fountain will naturally gush out the water of life, it will flow over the surface, and as a result, the forces present will absorb this energy, I have had revelations of this fountain being created in other locations in our solar system, and this causing great changes.

A river is never the same when you throw a stone into it, the water will never be the same, the smallest attitude taken at any one moment in your life can bring about the greatest existential changes in your journey.

May the heavenly forces bless you greatly.

Ars Aurora.

Final notes

My approach is quite peculiar as you may have read in this book, one of my life missions is to bring healing to this world, and this small and at the same time big book, is a way in which I can be passing on this knowledge, and assist in the journey of all the spirits of this earth.

There are no limitations to whom the water of life, oil, candle and celestial incense can be offered, if the spirit accepts, offer it very willingly, and as said before, be it angel, daimon, "demon", gods and goddesses from different pantheons and different cultures, ancestors, guides, orixás and the like.

The power of kindness, of healing, of love and mercy are universal, and echo throughout the cosmos, and also, manifest themselves through loving gestures like this, so these techniques are universal and are not attached to any entity or angel.

Even if the spirit of your cult, is already someone evolved or totally healed, you must offer the water of life, because the spirit can use this water to heal other spirits or people he wishes, regardless of who takes it, you will have started a healing process, and thus, you will be putting in process an infinite effect of enlightenment.

Clearly, this is a process, so always offer and do your conjurations and Blessings in all your rituals, in time, you will have brought about a gigantic change in the existence of the one you, with your small gesture of love, have offered the water of life to.

Thank you for purchasing an official copy of this book, it motivates me to bring more content and enables me to release new books with this theme, I hope you have great results and can change your life for the better, if you want to send me a feedback, opinion, or if you found any errors in the book, send me an email to: arsaurorayhvh@gmail.com

Remember to rate the book on amazon or whatever official platform you have purchased it from, your stars and comments are extremely important to me.

Thank you and see you soon <3

Printed in Great Britain
by Amazon